Navigating Life

With Confidence

Helping You to Thrive in Live by Growing from Within. Boosting Your Confidence and Self-Esteem

Bernie Egerton

Copyright © 2023 Bernie Egerton

All rights reserved.

This book is a holistic approach and does not replace the advice of a medical professional
ISBN:979-8-3985-5557-8

For Chris, Isla, and Kiera.
My world.

"Who looks outside dreams,

who looks inside awakes."

-Carl Jung

Navigating Life

With Confidence

Contents

Introduction   1

Part 1 - Emotions and Behaviours

1 Understanding Your Emotions   9
2 Why Perfectionism Can be Exhausting   21
3 Learning to Say No and Improving Assertiveness   27
4 Managing Stress and Grabbing Plenty of ZZZ   33
5 Let's Talk About Social Media   39

Part 2 - Growing from Within

6 Self-Care and the Power of Kindness   45
7 Growth Mindset & Igniting That Fire from Within   51
8 Motivation, Discipline and Self Belief   59
9 A Bit of Humour to Spark Those Moments of Joy   65

Part 3 - Relaxation and Mindfulness

10 Minfulness, Nature and Visualization Exercises   71

Part 4 - Letting Your Creative Juices Take Over

11 Nurturing the Creative Mind and Gratitude   79

Survey, Doodle Sheets and Gratitude Entries   85

Conclusion   99

Acknowledgements   100
About the Author   101
References   103

Navigating Life

With Confidence

Helping You to Thrive in Live by Growing from Within. Boosting Your Confidence and Self-Esteem

Introduction

When you doubt yourself and struggle with low self-esteem - you can be hard on yourself to the point where moving out of your comfort zone can feel like the most daunting/terrifying task. I was hard on myself. I still can be. However, it was the perfectionist in me that contributed massively towards my lack of confidence.

Having struggled with low self-esteem throughout my life, I've now learned how to step back while being more in tune with my emotions. I'm at a stage in life where I believe in myself and have accepted who I am as a person by being my authentic self. It's about self-awareness. Heck, being a Libra I'm all about working with those scales every single day.

Aiming to listen to your body as you question your own thoughts, by using tools provided throughout this book can help bring your own passions to fruition.

My aim is to help you to thrive. However, it does take time as it's about believing in yourself and your abilities. You always have choices in this life, and working on your own growth can help you to discover/work on your strengths - while gaining that confidence needed in moving forward. Believing how capable you really are.

Acceptance

Life can be hard, unfair, challenging, beautiful and amazing. It's accepting that life is one mountain climb (with plenty of splinters along the way). Plus, we're all vulnerable individuals in this life who have good and bad days, and that's ok, as you're only human.

Navigating that gigantic ocean by learning to ride those waves can make you stronger, and you will eventually tread that water with confidence.

If something is causing you stress or you lack the confidence to share how you are truly feeling: then using a coach or a therapist (to address deep rooted problems) can really help with your own personal growth. It helped me to look from within, to work on deep rooted issues and to grow as an individual. Even speaking to a family member or a friend who you trust or feel comfortable with can help to let it all out. It's good to talk. It really is.

Think of this book as your own personal mindset coach with thought-provoking questions, research, fun writing activities and relaxation techniques to help you to look from within. If it's easier highlight/bookmark sections that speak to you, and always keep an open mind.

An understanding of emotions and why you have limiting beliefs, will help you to dig that little bit deeper. This book will also give you tips and guidance on how to manage those stress levels during challenging times.

Pandemic and Appreciating the Simple Things

Look at the Covid Pandemic: now that was one curveball that opened our eyes well and truly up to what was important. It gave you time to reflect on life. It certainly made me more grateful for my family. It helped me to nurture my creative side and to work on my self-esteem. I also started appreciating nature and being present - while not stressing about things that are out of my control. It showed me the simple joys in life, such as the power of music. Especially showing that kitchen who rocked, while throwing about crazy moves to eighties/nineties music with the kids during those endless days in lockdown. Not taking myself too seriously! It can go an exceptionally long way when you learn to appreciate the simple things in life.

Throughout this book I will also be talking to you about mindfulness and the importance of tuning into your surroundings by using your **five** senses (what you **see, hear, feel, taste** and **smell**). You'll also see my poetry dotted throughout this book too, and how introducing gratitude/journaling into your life as a therapeutic outlet, can be beneficial for your mental wellbeing.

Do you want to thrive in life?

With an open mind, this coaching guide can help you to discover the brilliant, wonderful person that YOU truly are.

A Little Survey to Begin With

The following quick survey is a starting point to check in with yourself and how you're feeling at present. The same survey will be shared again at the end of this book – to monitor your progress.

1. **Do you have enough time to spend on what makes you feel happy?**

   o Yes
   o No

2. **What gives you the most joy?**

   o Time with family and friends
   o Exercising
   o Hobbies
   o Relaxing
   o Outdoors/Nature

3. **Do you lie awake worrying at night?**

   o Yes
   o No

4. **Do you get 7- 9hrs sleep each night?**

   o Yes
   o No

5. **Do you find time to relax?**

   o Yes
   o No

6. **How satisfied are you with your life at the moment?**

   o Satisfied
   o Dissatisfied

7. **Do you find it difficult asking for help if you are struggling?**

   o Yes
   o No

8. **Do you set goals?**

   o Yes
   o No

9. **Does moving out of your comfort zone make you feel uneasy?**

    o Yes
    o No

10. **What stops you from moving forward/making changes in your life?**

    o Fear
    o Lack of confidence

Having conducted my own research on over one hundred (anonymous) people:

- 70% responded with lack of confidence stopping them moving forward.
- 59% responded to not asking for help when needed.
- 61% said family and friends brought them the most joy.

"A journey of a thousand miles starts with a single step."

-Lao Tzu

Part 1
Emotions and Behaviours

1

Understanding Your Emotions

What first comes to mind when you think about emotions?
Maybe happiness is what you think, making you beam with pride as you think of the little joys in your life. On the other hand, however, it could be sadness, anger or fear that makes you feel anxious and uncertain about what the future holds. Emotions are part of who we are - it's our makeup.

Back in the 1970s, Psychologist Dr Paul Ekman who is widely known as an expert in facial expressions, studied and discovered how all human beings from every culture expressed the same seven facial expressions, which are called micro expressions (happiness, anger, fear, contempt, disgust, sadness, and surprise). According to Dr Ekman, he believed that studying the emotions of others from this non-verbal means of communication helped to understand how a person was actually feeling.

However, you might be good at reading the emotions of others due to having a sensitive personality and nervous system – where you absorb that energy around you.

Primary and Secondary Emotions

Primary and Secondary emotions dates back to 1980 by psychologist Robert Plutchik, who created the 'wheel of emotions' to describe how emotions are related. Becoming familiar with these terms can help you identify with what you are feeling, why you are feeling a certain way and how best to respond. You are taking a step back to really think about how you behave. Being more in tune with your emotions.

Primary Emotions

These are the first emotions you feel in any given situation and what you are born with.

Secondary Emotions

Our emotional responses to the primary emotions.

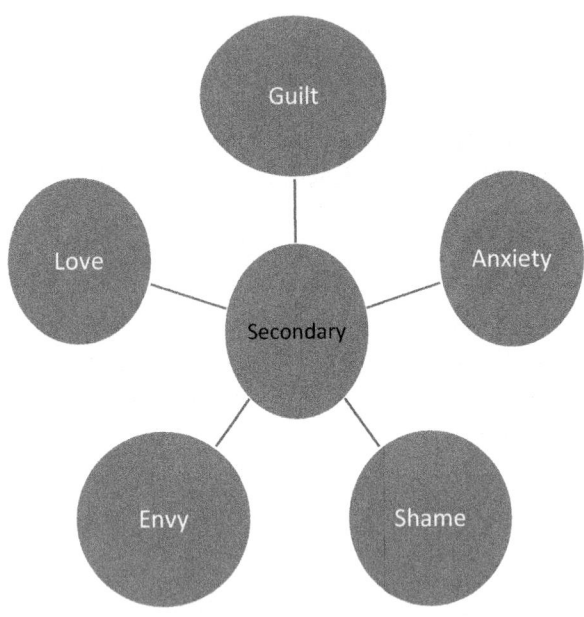

Examples of Primary and Secondary Emotions Working Together

- When experiencing fear **(primary)** - the **secondary** response could be anxiety (feeling flustered, have heart palpitations and panic attacks). I can certainly feel flustered with a racing heart coming up to presentations, job interviews or exams.

- Anger **(primary)** - you may feel a sense of shame or guilt **(secondary).** Guilt kicks in if I shout at my children or if I say something hurtful towards a member of my family. Recognising this, stepping back - asking myself "how could I have reacted differently and why was I feeling this way" always helps when working from within and being self-aware. You are taking a step back and acknowledging the actual experience.

Anger is part of being human. However, it's how you deal with anger and become aware of it, that can help you control this primary emotion.

Deep breath work or going for a long stroll surrounded by nature, really helps should I ever feel a little irritable/angry, and also during times of anxiety. It can be a great tool for relaxing - while also reflecting on the experience when in a calmer state.

Conscious, Preconscious and Unconscious Mind

Are you familiar with Sigmund Freud's Iceberg Model of Consciousness?

The model shows how the **mind** has **three** levels of **consciousness**.

- ❖ Imagine the **conscious** mind being the tip of an iceberg (current thought process, analytical thinking, aware of now, feelings of pain and our five senses).
- ❖ Think of the **preconscious** mind (mid-level) as retrievable stored memories - such as addresses, phone numbers, dates of birth or what you had for lunch, etc.
- ❖ The **unconscious** mind (bottom of iceberg) is where everything experienced through your life is stored (regrets, trauma, your beliefs, fears and anxieties).

Achieving your goals or passions in life can be challenging when you have negative beliefs that are deep rooted in the unconscious mind (the larger part of that iceberg that floats below the water). Hence, the famous saying "that's only the tip of the iceberg" when explaining an individual's behaviour. However, you can change your thought process with practice.

A little example:

I used to have a terrible fear of public speaking and would try to avoid it at all costs during work presentations, or when reading my own poetry to a live audience. Why was this? When I was about 10 years of age, I was asked to stand up in class to answer a question (I went red with embarrassment, and gosh did I feel that burn). I vividly remember two pupils laughing. It then followed me through life every time I would stand up to talk: triggering that memory (with that glow on my face) from my **unconscious** mind (bottom of iceberg). However, once I reframed my thought process, relaxed before each speaking event, and just took my time (without going like the bloody clappers) it made the experience easier each time I spoke. I kept practicing in front of smaller groups to improve my public speaking skills. Feeling a little nervous is healthy. However, you know it's time to address those negative beliefs when it interferes with your life. When you have deep-rooted negative beliefs about yourself and the world around, it can make reaching your full potential harder.

Four Examples of Changing Your Negative Beliefs

1. Negative belief:

"I'm so annoyed at myself for getting it wrong. I'm not good enough."

Change your inner dialogue to something like:

"It's ok to make mistakes. I'm only human."

2. Negative belief:

"I didn't get that job/job promotion. I didn't deserve it"

Change your inner dialogue to:

"I will ask for feedback in the areas I struggled with."

3. **Negative belief**:

"I hate public speaking for fear of being judged."

Change your inner dialogue to:

"I will practice in smaller groups and work with a coach/mentor to build on my confidence."

4. **Negative belief**:

"I'm not confident enough to join in on conversations to share my views."

Change your inner dialogue to:

"It's ok to join in and share my own views that are valid."

Exercise

Try to think of a few negative/core beliefs you have about yourself. How can you make your self-talk kinder?

Negative belief:

_____

Change inner dialogue to:

_____

Negative belief:

_____

Change inner dialogue to:

_____

Summary

An awareness of your primary and secondary emotions can help you to understand a little more about your behaviours and why you respond to situations the way you do.

Changing your negative/core beliefs can make your self-talk kinder, as you're giving yourself the permission to learn and grow (I will talk to you more about a growth mind-set later on in the book). You are helping yourself along that path of believing in yourself and your worth.

The more you practice changing the narrative and being aware of your negative thoughts, then it will become easier over time. It does take time. However, you will get there when working on yourself. Keep practicing and always go at a pace that feels comfortable to you. Keep building that toolkit up!

2

Why Perfectionism Can Be Exhausting

"One who fears failure limits his activities."

-Henry Ford

Jeepers, the amount of pressure we put on ourselves to do well and at such a high standard can be damaging to our wellbeing. Causing so much stress.

Back when I was studying; coming up to assignment deadlines was always an emotional nightmare. I would chop and change my work so bloody much, and my goodness it was never ending at the beginning of my studies. Then procrastination would kick in big time. How did procrastination show up you might be thinking? I would always go on a mad cleaning spree before eventually hitting that submit button.

Procrastination was in full force, my self-esteem would take a blow like nobody's business and those stress levels were raised.

Why was I feeling this way? It was fear of failing or doing absolutely rubbish. I would get flustered, and my head would be swimming with self-doubt. I didn't believe in my abilities.

Are you putting pressure on yourself to do well and at such a high standard? Failing is part of the learning process, but when you're a perfectionist it is so hard to view that outlook on life. However, making mistakes is part of being human.

Furthermore, maybe you are a person that wants everything to be perfect, chopping/changing what you've written over and over again as that little seed of doubt lingers and those weeds start to sprout big time. Causing havoc in your daily life. Pleasing everyone to seem like this perfect friend, person (when deep down you are struggling and ignoring how you really feel). You are an all or nothing type of person, and this can be absolutely exhausting. Heck, we all have flaws, but when you're a perfectionist it never feels good enough does it?

Be kind with your self-talk, become more aware of how you criticise yourself, and this will help you on that path of not torturing yourself.

On the other hand, however, perfectionism can be seen as a positive. Heck yes, it can make you one determined so and so and a very disciplined one at that.

However, studies suggest how perfectionism can cause problems such as headaches, binge eating, low self-esteem and anxiety.

Research on 41,641 American, Canadian, and British college students, stated a rise in perfectionism since the 2000s, due to young individual's living in an environment where the pressure of doing well was so high - with many suffering from depression and anxiety, and also how parents are more controlling than before*. This is no surprise really with social media now being a huge part of our lives, where the perfect life can be shown on these platforms every single day. It can be packed with people's achievements, wins and accomplishments: causing a huge amount of pressure for individuals.

Perfectionism Is Increasing Over Time: A meta-analysis study of birth cohort differences from Thomas Curran and Andrew Hill from 1989-2016 on college students.

How Can You Find That Right Balance?

Getting the balance right on those scales can take time. However, when you're focused on your own personal growth and wanting to change - then you can tame perfectionism to a manageable level.

Aim to learn from your mistakes, move on and take feedback as a positive for future assignments, work projects, training sessions or whatever you need to improve on. If you need to brush up on your talents: learn more about your craft and set realistic targets. Join a community of like-minded people.

Introducing affirmations into your daily life is a wonderful way to boost your confidence and to check in with yourself**.

If you are really struggling to manage your emotions where perfectionism has such a grip and is affecting your life - then working with a CBT therapist can really help to gain that clarity needed***.

Perfectionism and being confident with your work (while still working hard at something) are quite different.
When you're confident you can do a decent job, you work hard, and you believe in yourself. You don't overthink things

to the point of disaster. Furthermore, you are being kind with your self-talk. Remember to always be kind with your self-talk. If it doesn't go as planned - you learn/grow and it will all come to fruition.

It's ok to make mistakes. If you don't fail, how do you learn for next time?

**Affirmations are sayings you can repeat to yourself on a daily basis to boost confidence and self-worth. A few examples:
"I am relaxed, focused and in control." "I am confident." I am enough."
"I have the ability to achieve what I put my mind to."

*** Cognitive Behavioural Therapy is a form of therapy that uses problem solving skills to change thinking patterns. It focuses on an individual's present situation, in order to move forwards in their life and to cope with demanding situations.

3

Learning to Say No and Improving Assertiveness

Why is saying that two letter word always so difficult? Do you find it hard saying no? Leading to overwhelm from putting other people's needs before your own?

When I reflect on a time to who I was 10 years ago, I feel slightly embarrassed. Why? I was a people pleaser. However, the beauty about writing this - is acknowledging the fact of how far I've come. Back in my people pleasing days and not being able to say no - was down to my lack of assertiveness. I didn't want to be portrayed as rude or unkind. Do you relate to this? Exhausting, isn't it?

Overcoming People Pleasing

How do you learn to say no? Am I now an expert in saying no? Absolutely not. However, I do say it with confidence if it doesn't suit - without the need of a long-winded explanation where it feels like you're explaining yourself for eternity. When all you had to say was that two-letter word in a diplomatic manner.

You can't say no all the time. It's what suits you. If you listen to your gut and know it doesn't feel right, then it's ok for you to set those healthy boundaries and say no.

The one person who needs your approval most is yourself. Start working on that relationship.

When I look back on a time where I was a big *people pleaser, I wasn't aware I was doing it and thought it was normal practice to get people to like you. Seeking approval.

After having my own coaching, I then slowly gained that confidence and belief in myself. I started to put my own needs at the top of that pile every single time. It's not selfish putting your own needs first - it's empowering and how you become the best version of yourself for you and your loved ones!

---

*People pleasing can be draining. Learning to say no can help build on your assertiveness over time, while also reducing those stress levels.

Six Tips to Help Say No - Without Feeling Guilty and Stressed to the Hilt

1. Work on yourself, listen to your gut and take your time.

2. Practice mindfulness/meditation to connect with your inner self. I'm a firm believer in mindfulness and being present. With that self-awareness you tap right into your inner voice. Building on your confidence.

3. Journal. It can be a great tool for writing down those thoughts/emotions. It might seem hard at the beginning to write from such a raw place, but you begin to learn so much about yourself.

4. Practice breathing techniques. A great tool for stepping back and reconnecting with yourself.

5. Work with a mentor or attend workshops focused on confidence building.

6. Remember - assertiveness is not being rude. Saying no in a diplomatic manner can help with your own growth going forward.

Summary

Learning to say no can seem challenging at the beginning, but the more you say it, the easier it gets over time and the less stressed/anxious you'll become. Assertiveness will then grow. Start off slowly, so you can build yourself up to saying it with ease. If it suits, then great say yes, if it doesn't then say no.
People pleasing is a trait many people have, for others saying no is so much easier.
Remember to look out for you first. The more you work on yourself; then learning to say no and not pleasing others will become easier. It's about finding that right balance. Growing, learning, self-awareness and building yourself up. Growth is a constant journey.
When you start loving yourself more, then low self-esteem will drift further away as that little seed starts to flourish. Water it with kindness and watch it grow.

I still work with a mentor to help during times when I need a bit more clarity, so to be the best person, parent and coach - as well as respecting my emotional wellbeing.

4

Managing Stress and Grabbing Plenty of ZZZ

On a scale from 1-10 how are your stress levels at the moment? With 1 being completely chilled and 10 being stressed to the hilt. Try to be honest with yourself as it's always good to be in tune with how you feel: then circle the scale below.

1 2 3 4 5 6 7 8 9 10

Ask yourself these questions:

- ❖ How is my diet?
- ❖ What amount of sleep do I get every night?
- ❖ What changes (if any) are going on in my life?
- ❖ Do I get enough exercise/time outdoors.
- ❖ How much water do I drink each day?

According to the Mental Health Foundation UK - 74% of adults had felt stressed and overwhelmed in 2018. This online study was one of their largest on stress with 4,619 respondents. Also, at the time of writing this (2023) the cost-of-living crisis was causing so much stress for everyone. Looking after your health and well-being is more important than ever.

What is Stress and How to Keep it Under Control

Stress is when your body goes into the fight and flight mode - as a result your cortisol levels go up. Cortisol is the main stress hormone that works with certain parts of your brain to control your mood. It also increases blood sugar and regulates blood pressure (Holford, 2007). Having a poor diet, being an over thinker, working in an unhealthy environment or relationship struggles; can make you more prone to stress. Being stressed can really take its toll on the body - making the risks higher for blood pressure, heart disease, digestive problems and many more problems.

Six Tips to Help Keep Stress at Bay

- Exercising regularly regulates blood sugar and lowers those cortisol levels (even a long walk-in nature or a swim. It doesn't have to be strenuous).
- Sleep is the foundation to a healthier life and keeping stress at bay. Aiming for an earlier night's sleep is key (at least 7 hrs).
- Eating healthy foods like fruits, green leafy veg, eggs, yoghurt, wholemeal instead of white, nuts, meat, and oily seafood, can reduce stress. You can also introduce a good multivitamin.
- Aim to drink plenty of water throughout the day, keeping you hydrated and focused.
- Journaling can also help to release any tension you may be feeling and to make sense of things (really works wonders putting pen to paper to release stress). Even keeping a diary to make a note of important appointments can release any overwhelm. You're not worrying about forgetting dates.
- Avoid caffeine just before bed and take a break from social media if it affects your mood as that can be a big one.

I know I'm feeling stressed when the palpitations/butterflies start as I'm about to fall asleep at night (I avoid caffeine before bed.) I start to feel irritable, tired, not myself, and those beautiful little bad boys called 'cold sores' can make an appearance too. I know it's time to slow down and look after my body when any of these familiar symptoms appear. Getting a proper night's sleep is key (it's a ritual for me to get at least 7hrs sleep every night).

Coming up to exams, job interviews, being a parent or juggling lots of balls can all contribute to stress. On the other hand, however, stress can work in your favour throughout certain times of your life. A little stress can be healthy. You can perform better; switching to auto pilot and can get the job done should it be right before an exam, reaching a work deadline, preparing for sports events or situations where you need to be focused. A little stress can help you during certain times as you want to perform at your best. Adrenaline is what gives us that boost. Sometimes you might feel invincible when stress hits: giving you that final push to reach the finishing line like a pro. However, it's being aware when your body is feeling the pinch.

Try the following breathing exercise. It's as a great tool for relieving any stress/anxiety you may be feeling.

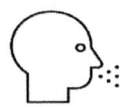

➢ *Inhale slowly through your nose for 5 seconds*
➢ *Hold for 5 seconds*
➢ *Exhale slowly through the mouth for 5 seconds.*
➢ *Repeat until you feel relaxed/calmer.*

Summary

Remember: a proper night's sleep, being mindful, your diet and exercising are all key to reducing stress.

Although a certain level of stress can be healthy and help you to perform better; becoming mindful should it reach a level where it starts to affect your daily life is a great start in being self-aware. I would also like to add that I'm not a nutritionist – however I'm sharing what I've learned/studied to date.

5

Let's Talk About Social Media

You're scrolling, having a harmless browse - next thing you know you're scrolling for eternity. You're checking out profiles, switching to autopilot, making yourself feel worse – then lo and behold you're sucked right down that bloody rabbit hole.

With social media now being a big part of our lives, we have so much information that is just a click away - at our fingertips. It's no surprise we become overwhelmed and lose confidence in ourselves with an abundance of information. Scrolling is great exercise for your thumb, but not your brain. Nowadays, we compare our lives to others and our confidence dips.

It's not surprising why you feel bad after a browsing session when it comes to social media. Selfies are everywhere, filters are on hand, those perfect (well edited) life snaps are shown and the "like" button has become gold dust to many people.

God help it if you don't like that photo or status update, and let's not forget about those keyboard warriors. It's the way life has become. The list is endless.

On the other hand, however, social media can be a wonderful place for promoting your business, learning about your craft, sharing your creativity, showing the funniest of videos and raising awareness on important causes/subjects.

You're in a time where everything is done online and working from home is more common since the pandemic. Being mindful when online is a step to being more in control.

My Own Relationship with Social Media

When I first became acquainted with social media back in 2007, I have to admit I loved it. Social media was a new way to connect with others, and I thought it was the best thing since sliced bread! It was such a novelty. I loved checking into places, posting the obligatory holiday snaps and sharing the snaps I 'wanted' the world to see. My goodness did that soon change. I started comparing my life to others (especially if I was having a crap day) and the perfectionist in me felt worse.

When I look back and reflect on that time, social media wasn't healthy for my emotional well-being. When the novelty of this new toy had worn off, my self-esteem dipped, and I wasn't self-aware.

Do you find your mood changing when you're scrolling? Just have a think about that for a minute.

How does social media really make you feel? Is it worth the amount of time you spend on it?

I remember well before mobiles, the Internet and managed quite well. I was brought up in the country during the eighties, and spending time outdoors playing games, running wild in those fields was my social media.

In today's world, don't you feel lost if your phone isn't attached to those hands? It's like something awful has happened if you leave the house and realise your pocket/bag is missing the device. God help it if you lose it. I bet you've pulled that sofa apart searching for it? I've been there.

I'm more mindful these days with social media after removing my personal social media accounts years ago. Being truthful, I had to for my emotional wellbeing (I feel more content and it's an awful procrastination tool).

However, I still have social media, but more for hobbies/work. Furthermore, maybe you do have control when it comes to social media for your personal use and that's great. It's about being mindful when using a social media platform. You're in a time where social media is so powerful and addictive (jeepers it can be addictive). Try not to compare your life (I know it's easier said than done) as you're unique and brilliant in your own ways.

Statistics

- Research has shown how 45% of adolescents have reported to being online "almost constantly."
- 44% stated being online several times a day*. This is a huge percentage of younger people spending their time online on a daily basis - and is bound to impact mental health.
- However, a survey report has shown how 31% of adolescents found social media use as a positive experience due to connecting with others*.
- Furthermore, 25% of adolescents found social media to have such a negative impact*.

Researchers have also shown how social media can disrupt sleep. I can vouch for this myself as I used to take my phone to bed (I stopped that years ago) pop it under my pillow, and if I woke during the night - would have a quick check then the dreaded scrolling would start.

Leave your phone downstairs at night or put it away, in order to get that proper night's sleep your body and mind craves.

National Center For Health Research (2018) 'Social Media and Adolescents' and Young Adults Mental Health.

Final Takeaway on Managing Social Media

There are positives to using social media when you become aware when browsing. If you find yourself feeling low after spending quite a bit of time scrolling, then take a step back. Go easy on yourself and ask yourself: what is making me feel like this when online?

Follow accounts that make you feel good. If you find it gets a bit too much, then taking a little break from it can be healthy to focus on other things. You could dedicate a day with no social media use every week or aim to set yourself a time limit when online. Start a hobby you enjoy. Channel your energies into what makes you smile. Taking a step back from the device by going outdoors and spending time in nature to recharge your batteries can be so beneficial. Breathe in that fresh air, absorb the present moment. Become more aware of your feelings when scrolling. Check in with yourself. Ask yourself "do I feel ok doing this"? You are more than enough - you really are. I feel much happier not having a personal social media account and I limit my time spent when browsing on the phone.

Talk to someone if it gets a bit too much. It's ok to share how you're feeling with someone you trust – it's not a weakness but very much a strength to open up.

Part 2

Growing From Within

6

Self-Care and the Power of Kindness

Self-care is an expression thrown around so much these days, isn't it? However, it really is a practice to incorporate into your daily life. Even 20 minutes to grab some you time!
For me, I feel so much better after a 30-minute walk surrounded by nature, should it be in the park or anywhere with plenty of greenery. I enjoy walking in a nice quiet environment as I always feel refreshed, and it clears my mind. Walking is also a fantastic way to spark inspiration for the creatives. Throughout a walk it gives me time to reflect on things, to admire the beauty of nature and to just be with me.

If you work in an office, even taking a 15-minute walk outside for fresh air during lunch can make all the difference. It's about getting into a little routine.

Self-care can mean absolutely anything. It can be sitting reading an enjoyable book uninterrupted for 20-30 minutes, it can be playing your favourite instrument, meditating, going for a swim, or hitting that gym! Even something as simple as taking time out to enjoy your favourite cup of tea/coffee without the rushing about. Boy, do I love sitting down with that obligatory chai latte and sipping it uninterrupted (a joy when you're a parent). Something so simple can be powerful when you let it! Anything that makes you feel happier/relaxed.

Dedicating Time for You

Starting a bit of self-care that focuses on your needs should become priority - as we live in a world where life can be so busy. And we often forget to put our own needs first. The pandemic made us realise how much we do rush about. If you are in a constant state of 'rush' then you will find it hard to focus on what you really want/need. Even 20 minutes each day will make all the difference as you are becoming aware of your needs. After a while it will become habitual. You are focusing on building a healthier relationship with yourself.

Remember: you are always priority and taking that time out to practice self-care every day is so important for your physical and emotional well-being.

The Power of Kindness

"My religion is very simple.
My religion is kindness."

-*Dalai Lama*

Kindness to others and being kind to yourself really is the way to make the world a kinder place, isn't it? It makes you feel good when you're being kind. Spreading kindness and receiving kindness can work wonders for your self-worth. It's a topic that comes up often during coaching sessions. Should it be random acts of kindness, volunteering to help those in need or giving someone that extra bit of support when needed. It really does bring a smile to your face. Kindness leaves an imprint so big on people's hearts.

I wrote the following poem during the pandemic to highlight the power of kindness. During dark and challenging times, a little kindness goes such a long way. Kindness always prevails.

Thank You, it's Nice to Be Kind

A gentle smile, a heartfelt word, clears the cloud from my mind. Lifting me out of the darkest of places 'thank you' it's nice to be kind.
A little text with those words 'I'm here' travels the length of the earth. The racing mind slowly calms from every word and its worth.

In a world portraying so much anger yet still has so much beauty - spreading kindness every day is undoubtedly everyone's duty.
Be kind you say, how hard is this in a world with so much confusion?
Kindness helps one another without the fear and intrusion.

To someone in need a simple hello or even a chat over tea - is the greatest gift to make a person thrive and somewhat feel free.
A withered flower blossom's again and is no longer blind.
Lifting me out of the darkest of places, 'thank you' it's nice to be kind.

7

A Growth Mindset and Igniting That Fire from Within

"Your vision will become clear only when you can look into your own heart. Who looks outside, dreams; who looks inside, awakes."

- Carl Jung

During a wonderful coaching session with a client one time, it helped me to focus more on my own passions and strengths when listening to them open up about what brought so much joy to their lives. I always enjoy seeing people's faces light up when they speak about their true passions in life and from the heart.

- What are you passionate about?
- What ignites that fire inside you?

I know myself when I'm enthusiastic about something it makes me feel whole, confident, and capable. When you focus too much on your weaknesses and try to do it all, then lo and behold self-doubt pops right back up to say "here I am" trying to make you think otherwise. Life really is short - the more you spend worrying and doubting your capabilities, the more stressed you become. Avoiding following your true path in life. As I mentioned earlier - baby steps. Take your time to grow, believe in yourself and work from within.

Growth Mindset

When you have a growth mind-set you are always looking at ways to improve yourself, your talents: and you learn from your mistakes. You're a sucker for learning new things and you're not being too hard on yourself during the process either.

Are you hard on yourself if things don't go as planned? Therefore, spending forever overthinking the situation, beating yourself up as your confidence plummets.
I used to believe if I wasn't good at something, then that was it (fixed mind-set).

However, with a growth mind-set I reflect on situations, write in my journal (to process) have my own coaching (to gain clarity and grow), take courses (learning) and I practice gratitude (there is power in being grateful for the simple things in life).

I'm constantly learning and brushing up on my skills to become better. Don't get me wrong, there are days where low self-worth comes knocking right on my door. Of course it does. I answer it, listen to it and question it.

However, I don't spend time dwelling or entertaining those thoughts as I'm self-aware in comparison to how I used to be.

Personal development is so important and can be part of your daily life going forward. You learn, progress, reflect and grow every single day.

- ❖ What areas need training/improving in your life?
- ❖ How can you banish those limiting beliefs?
- ❖ What little acts makes you feel positive?
- ❖ What are your core values?

Jumping Out of Your Comfort Zone

Are you afraid to jump out of your comfort zone, in order to take on new challenges? Do you feel you're not good enough and want to play it safe? Fear of the unknown can stop us from taking that step forward and to reach our goals/passions in life. Jumping out of your comfort zone, eliminating that fear, and making decisions: although it may feel uncomfortable, could be life changing.

Build it Up Slowly

When you set goals, a solid plan needs to be in place written down - within a realistic time. Start off slowly and at a pace that suits you. Do all that inner work, while getting to know your strengths/weaknesses and what drives you!

Step By Step Process

When I set my own goals, I am more focused/clear when I do it step by step. Sometimes you can get too carried away – wanting the whole shebang overnight, where your head feels like it's going to explode. All these incredible thoughts, ideas running around in your mind. The next thing you know you're overwhelmed and that confidence dips.

My goodness does it dip. When it gets to that stage, step back and ask yourself these questions.

- ❖ What is my plan?
- ❖ How can I make this achievable?
- ❖ How can I do this in a manageable way?
- ❖ What is stopping me from moving forward right now?

Set realistic goals, then reassess over time. And, if you're reaching those targets, then aim higher - go for it. Do it. It really is all in the planning.

Using the SMART Guide to Help with Setting Goals!

When setting goals, I like to use the following **SMART** guide to help me throughout the goal setting process.

Specific

Measurable

Attainable

Realistic

Time-band

Summary

Each step forward counts - sometimes taking a step back to recharge those batteries to reconnect with yourself, can make a difference. You're raring to go again. Go easy on yourself. Set realistic goals. Slow and steady wins the race – look what happened to that poor hare. We all go at our own pace. Always listen to your gut and take your time. You hold that key firmly in your hands. Unlock that wonderful door. You are more than capable. Go for it!

8

Motivation, Discipline and Self Belief

How do you start your day?

In the morning when I get up with the kids, I make the beds and open those blinds/curtains - to let all that brightness in. Do you know something? I feel better, less stressed, and relaxed. Starting the day on a positive note. It gives me that kick start I need.

I also get myself up earlier when getting the kids ready for school. Do you give yourself that little bit of breathing space each morning? Otherwise, you're rushing about like a headless chicken, the feathers are ruffled and the stress levels rise. Creating a more relaxed, stress free, healthier morning routine can really set you up for the day.

An earlier bedtime routine each night can help too, so you have that extra time each morning - as well as feeling rested.

When you start your day motivated and relaxed, then it follows through for the rest of that day, making you more productive at work. The smallest of changes can make such an enormous difference and you're learning to manage those stress levels too.

Self-Belief and Hard Work to Reach That Finishing Line

I ran and completed two marathons in 2010 and 2013. How did I feel? Delighted, relieved, exhausted, sore, but proud. How did I make it happen? For each marathon I spent four solid months training 6 days per week and booked 5k/10k races as part of my training plan.

I followed a great marathon book (that book was my training and nutrition coach). I also trained with my dear friend (shout out to Jane) who was a great support throughout. Having a training buddy is great motivation, plus you don't want to let them down and vice versa!

When reflecting - it was extremely challenging work and there were times where I wanted to give up, shed tears and my confidence was knocked. However, I always focused on the end goal as I visualized myself running over that finishing line. Bloody hell did I keep that picture firmly in my mind.

When you set yourself a target - discipline is the main driver that helps you to achieve those goals along with motivation. I've always been a disciplined and motivated person. However, finding the right balance of staying disciplined and not being extremely hard on myself took a long time to accomplish. Working hard, believing in yourself and not being too hard on yourself are important when it comes to self-discipline. If it doesn't go to plan then step back, analyse, and visualize. Move forward with your goals or to plan B. When you train for a marathon you're following a set plan, and slowly building yourself up (both mentally and physically) to reach a certain standard. It's all in the preparation, planning and tweaking the schedule if it doesn't work out. Don't give up, focus, and act. Plus, there's always plan B to avoid any injuries

When you set goals and have a structured plan in place, then you begin to believe in yourself.

How to Get Motivation off to a Flying Start

- Use the **SMART** reference (page 54) to help with goal setting.
- Write down exactly what it is you want to achieve
- Set a time limit (3-6 months for example)
- Aim to get 7-9 hours sleep per night.
- Join groups/communities focused on those goals
- Go for a good long walk, to clear the head and to soak up nature for you to gain clarity
- Always focus on what YOU enjoy, to keep that momentum going!

Summary

What we feed ourselves mentally certainly affects our performance. When you put in the work, then you get results. It's all in the preparation, believing in yourself, doing the research, and being disciplined. Keep checking in with yourself, reflect throughout the process and be kind with your self-talk. It's so much easier when it's something you are enthusiastic about.

Running a marathon is HARD WORK. It's putting in the time and commitment where you build yourself up. You pace yourself.

I make sure I follow a plan, set goals, have a sharp vision, and I work bloody hard at what I set out to achieve.

Should you be training for a marathon, working towards a big job promotion, changing career, wanting to lose weight or anything that involves commitment - discipline, preparation, planning, and visualizing that end result will get you there. You can do whatever you put your mind to.

Believe in yourself, lace up those trainers and get starting.

9

A Bit of Humour to Spark Those Moments of Joy

*"Laugh as much as possible, always laugh.
It's the sweetest thing one can do for
oneself and one's fellow human beings."*
-Maya Angelou

Do you enjoy a bit of banter? Oh boy I certainly do. Sometimes it can turn sour moments into a bit of light-heartedness, and I come from a family where humour is very much used (plus I'm Irish). It's true when they say laughter is the best medicine, as it gives you that lift you sometimes need.

A Little Story

One cold and dreary wet day during the pandemic when knee deep doing the dishes with the hubby (and the lockdown malarkey was fairly losing its novelty). I started saying the famous quote to him by Elbert Hubbard 'when life gives you lemons make lemonade'. He quickly turned around, stopped me in my tracks (mid-sentence) and as calm as you like said "bite the f***ers." Well. I burst out laughing so hard. We both did (I hope this gave you a little giggle/smile too).

Sometimes, you have to turn daunting situations into humour, as you work through those sour pimpled bad boys: to see where those tangy pips and pulps end up!

The Pandemic was a big revelation to the power of humour as a coping mechanism. Peoples text messages, social media accounts and emails were inundated with funny videos, reels and poems. Spirits were being lifted during great sadness in our world, and it showed the importance of keeping that spark from within alive, while not taking things too seriously. It was bittersweet.

Even watching a good show. Schitts Creek was the lift I needed during the pandemic. It was a great form of escapism while the kids were tucked up in bed, as the hubby and I had a good night of belly laughing.

Research

Research has shown how laughter can make you perform better in the workplace: boosting creativity and problem-solving skills. It also shows how laughing together as a group can reduce anxiety levels (Daisley, B 2018). I know myself when I've bantered with work colleagues and family/friends it makes me forget about my worries. And, also when being completely silly/belly laughing with the kids!

Researchers have also shown how laughing can act as a natural pain killer; from the chemicals (endorphins) it releases during a good fit of laughter. Experimenters from Oxford University had split volunteers into two groups for testing pain thresholds*. One group watched comedy for 15 minutes as the other group watched dull videos for 15 minutes. In response to the experiment: respondents withstood 10% more pain from belly laughing than prior to watching comedy. On the other hand, however it showed how the respondents were less able to withstand pain after viewing the boring video*. This is remarkable really and not surprising: you're temporarily forgetting the pain (both mentally and physically) during a good bout of laughter.

***Pallab Ghosh, 2011 'study reveals laughter really is the best medicine'.*

"Enjoy life. Have fun. Be kind. Have worth. Have friends. Be honest. Laugh. Die with dignity. Make the most of it. It's all we've got."

-Ricky Gervais

Grabbing That Tonic

Try to watch your favourite comedy series, go to a stand-up gig, read a funny book, banter with family and friends, or turn to whatever gives you a good hearty belly laugh: on those days when all you want to do is have a good cry (which is healthy by the way) and a gin. So... When life gives you lemons: slice them, work with them, make lemonade or bite the f***ers.

Part 3

Mindfulness and Relaxation

10

Mindfulness, Nature, and Visualization Exercises

"To the mind that is still,
the whole universe surrenders."
-Lao Tzu

When life stood tragically still during Covid, I soaked up the outdoors and connected with nature and my family. We had the time to be still - appreciating the simple, yet most powerful things in life. The pandemic opened my eyes well and truly up to that.

I started to crave nature and became more self-aware. Realising that free stuff like fresh air, sunsets, birds chirping, mountains, and a beautiful garden are food for the soul.

Aiming to take time out for mindful moments can help to find that balance needed to reconnect with yourself.

Research from the Mental Health Foundation UK (2021) has shown how the more connected you are with nature then the happier you feel with yourself. Therefore, having a more positive impact on your emotional wellbeing. Figures showed 45% of individuals had felt more able to cope with the pandemic by spending time outdoors in nature.

Slowing Down

When you stop striving for perfection, you automatically slow down, realising that all that beauty was right under your nose (while your mind was busy from those to do lists and pleasing others). Self-awareness and being in the present moment can help you to become more confident.

When you stop worrying about what others think, then you start building on that relationship with yourself. You begin to grow more as a person. When fear no longer holds you back, you can take that step forward, achieving what your heart desires.

To have a stoic mindset means looking from within and being in tune with your emotional state; knowing who you are (without striving for more and wanting it all).

Adopting these principles can lead to making better decisions, feeling happier and gaining clarity. You're content with life, and the materialistic stuff goes straight to the bottom of that pile. It's like having the mindset of a monk. They really know how to take things in their stride!

For more on relaxation and hypnotherapy visit my website:

www.bernieegerton.com

Visualization Exercises

Visualization/relaxation exercises are helpful for being more present – it can help you to reach your goals in life. It can also help if you're having trouble relaxing or falling asleep at night.
Especially after a busy day. You can start off with a minute or two to begin with - building it up each day as you become more comfortable, relaxed, and focused. A bit like meditation.

Try to Visualize the Following Words Before Completing the Next Exercise (page 75)

There's something peaceful about the beach, being near the sea, listening to the swishing sound of the ocean as you dip your toes into that water. Sand is sinking beneath your grounded feet as the gentle breeze brushes against your cheeks. You can feel a sense of calm and connection to that beautiful environment as you soak up that tranquil scene. Watching the waves dancing with the sun as it sparkles like diamonds. And, relax.

Exercise

- ❖ Find a quiet place for you to focus/relax
- ❖ Concentrate on the beach image for a few moments - soaking up that calming scene. Absorb it. Feel it.
- ❖ Close your eyes
- ❖ Inhale deeply for 3 seconds
- ❖ Exhale slowly for 4 seconds (keep repeating until you feel calmer)
- ❖ Visualize the soothing swishing sound of the ocean and the calming sandy beach

Deep breaths, Visualize and Relax

Mindfulness Exercise

Next time you go for a walk, become more aware by using your **five** senses. Keep bringing yourself back to those senses if you feel your mind drifting (what you **see, hear, feel, taste** and **smell**). This can be a great exercise for being more in the moment and self-aware. You can even try this when washing dishes or sitting down. You are becoming aware of your body and living in the now.

- Look at your surroundings – what can you see?
- How does your body feel - is it relaxed, tense or painful?
- What can you smell?
- What can you hear?
- What can you touch - is it hot, smooth, cold?

I wrote the following poem after one of my mindful walks.

Lost in the Moment of Life and its Art

A flock of wild birds they fly in chilled air
I walk, embracing the earths open heart.

A seagull it sweeps, alone with no care -
lost in the moment of life and its art.

Bare trees that stand tall with nests where birds grew,
leaves lying crumpled and soggy from dew.

Clear beads as they rest on blades of green grass.
Autumn alive, soft clouds as they pass.

A squirrel it dances - I watch, he's aware,
its bushy long tail, he captures my stare.

This vision absorbed, the rush is no more,
nature alive unlocking my core.

Connections so strong I open my heart.
Lost in the moment of life and its art.

Part 4

Letting Your Creative Juices Take Over

11

Nurturing the Creative Mind and Gratitude

"Only in our creative acts do we step forth into the light and see ourselves whole and complete."

-Carl Jung

Creative writing is using your imagination to create poetry, short stories, and novels. Research has shown how writing can be a powerful tool to use when feeling overwhelmed. In the creative writing process, it uses the *five senses, **metaphor and ***simile throughout. It can boost your self-esteem as you're reaching from within to learn more about yourself - listening to your inner voice. Writing poetry certainly helped me through the pandemic, and to make sense of life during such a challenging time. Writing in free flow is a great means of expression. It's cathartic. Sometimes it's good to let all those thoughts that are swimming around in your mind, out onto that blank page.

In the following pages you will find word prompts and blank pages. Give the writing exercise a little go and set yourself a timer of 3 minutes (not thinking too much about the process).

Let those creative juices flow! Pick a word or two you are drawn to from the list and write what comes to mind.

Remember not to worry about it being perfect as you can always polish it off later. It's about being in the moment with your emotions. Feeling those words.

---

*Five senses. **See, hear, taste, touch,** and **smell**.

**A metaphor is used to describe a person or object to something with similar characteristics to add more power/emotion to your writing (showing and not telling). An example from my earlier poem: 'A withered flower blossoms again and is no longer blind.' (exhausted/stressed person finds a new lease of life)

***A simile is comparing one thing to another using 'as' or 'like.'
For example: 'As strong as an ox' 'As blind as a bat'

Word Prompts

Inner voice	Stillness	Calm
Change	Goals	Bare
Bloom	Focus	Navigate

Gratitude

Journaling and practicing gratitude is something you can introduce as part of your daily life, to focus on the positives. However, I know some days can be difficult to practice gratitude when you're not in the mood, or life just becomes too busy, where you have to dig that little bit deeper. However, research has shown how gratitude lists can have a positive impact to your mental wellbeing*. Focusing on the good in your life.

I started writing a journal during Covid, finishing each entry with three things I am grateful for and also a mood tracker for each entry. It can be a great stress management tool - for working on yourself, your beliefs and building on your confidence.

---

*The Therapeutic power of writing (2019) Available at: https://www.bbc.co.uk/bitesize/articles/zbty6v4

3 Tips to Help Incorporate Journaling and Gratitude into Your Life.

1. Invest in a good journal and write. It's good to let it out.

2. Write a list of 3-5 things you're grateful for each day - or even thinking about it as you wake up in the morning or before going to sleep at night. The simple things in life can make such a significant difference.

3. Date each entry into your journal and write down whatever mood you are feeling that day. If you are looking back over your journal, you can pinpoint what triggers certain moods - noticing a pattern. An example of a gratitude/mood entry is provided on the next page along with affirmations.

Date

Three things am I grateful for today

1. _____
2. _____
3. _____

Mood   I am feeling _____

Affirmation

"I am focused, confident and relaxed."

Chapter Summary

Creative writing or keeping a journal can be a wonderful way to focus on your inner voice. You are monitoring how you feel, and it makes you self-aware.

At the end of this book gratitude entries are provided for you to complete on a daily basis if you would like to give it a go. It's a great tool to introduce into your life: giving you that time to think about what makes YOU smile. And, how the smallest, yet powerful moments in life can spark that happiness from within.

Aim to give it a go. See how you feel after doing it for a few weeks. Invest in a little journal and download a free gratitude app (I love the happyfeed app) focused on gratitude lists.

Survey, Doodle Sheets and Gratitude Entries

As mentioned at the beginning of this book, I'm sharing the survey again - for you to check in with yourself and how you're progressing with your own growth. Always remember to take baby steps and each step forward counts - no matter how big or small! Slow and steady wins the race.

1. **Do you have enough time to spend on what makes you feel happy?**

    o   Yes
    o   No

2. **What gives you the most joy?**

    o   Time with family and friends
    o   Exercising
    o   Hobbies
    o   Relaxing
    o   Outdoors/Nature
    o   None of the above

3. **Do you lie awake worrying at night?**

    o   Yes
    o   No

4. **Do you get 7- 9hrs sleep each night?**

    o   Yes
    o   No

5. **Do you find time to relax?**

    o   Yes
    o   No

6. How satisfied are you with your life at the moment?

    o Satisfied
    o Dissatisfied

7. Do you find it difficult asking for help if you are struggling?

    o Yes
    o No

8. Do you set goals?

    o Yes
    o No

9. Does moving out of your comfort zone make you feel uneasy?

    o Yes
    o No

10. What stops you from moving forward/making changes in your life?

    o Fear
    o Lack of confidence

Doodle Sheets

Feel free to write, draw or doodle in the following pages and let those creative juices take over. I've also provided a few days of gratitude lists for you to complete on a daily basis too.

A reminder of creative writing terms/word prompts to help you with inspiration:

- Five senses. *See, hear, taste, touch, and smell.*

- Metaphor - used to describe a person or object to something with similar characteristics to add more power/emotion to your writing (showing and not telling). An example from my earlier poem: 'A withered flower blossoms again and is no longer blind.' (An exhausted person finds a new lease of life)

- Simile - is comparing one thing to another using 'as' or 'like:' i.e., 'as strong as an ox,' 'as blind as a bat, 'I ran like the wind'

Word Prompts

- Growth
- Stillness
- Confidence
- Breath
- Laughter
- Inner

Date

Three things am I grateful for today?

1. _____
2. _____
3. _____

Mood   I am feeling _____

Affirmation

I am relaxed, I am focused, I am always in control.

Date

Three things am I grateful for today?

1. _____
2. _____
3. _____

Mood   I am feeling _____

Affirmation (insert your own below)

Date

Three things am I grateful for today?

1. _____
2. _____
3. _____

Mood   I am feeling _____

Affirmation (insert your own below)

Date

Three things am I grateful for today?

1. _____
2. _____
3. _____

Mood   I am feeling _____

Affirmation (insert your own below)

Date

Three things am I grateful for today?

1. _____
2. _____
3. _____

Mood   I am feeling _____

Affirmation (insert your own below)

Conclusion

Thank you so much for buying my book and reading the content. I hope it has brought a bit of comfort/guidance to you. The tools provided within this book can help you on your own journey of growth going forward. I've shared what helps me on a daily basis to be a more confident person. My self-esteem has been boosted since becoming self-aware. Without that self-awareness and learnings to date I wouldn't be the person I am today. The journey from within and its lessons are endless - go with every step of that journey.

Remember: you always have a choice in this life. Be kind to yourself and believe in yourself - as you hold that key firmly in your hand. Once you start believing in your worth, then you can unlock that door to wonderful things. What you deserve. Life really is short. You deserve to live it to your full potential.

Acknowledgements

A massive thank you to my husband Chris who has always been so patient and supportive throughout the writing process: especially when I've doubted myself. To my little girls Isla and Kiera who make me so proud every day, and to be a better person.

To mum, dad, Peter and Joseph who have been there to give me that boost when needed! To my friends and extended family.

To Helena, Susan and Tiggie for the guidance/mentoring - it has been invaluable.

Thank you
xxx

About the Author

Bernie is a Mindset Coach, Clinical Hypnotherapist, Blogger and Writer. Having worked in the corporate world for 10 years, she followed her passion by changing career to help and coach others. She has worked in community outreach, volunteered for charities, and has written articles for wellbeing magazines.

In her spare time, she enjoys writing poetry, sketching and soaking up the outdoors with her family. She lives in England with her husband and their two little girls.

For more about Bernie and her coaching/workshop services - visit her website at:

www.bernieegerton.com
or
bernspoetry on Instagram for her poetry pieces

References

Chapter 1
Ekman, P (2023) 'Paul Ekmans Contribution to Society.'
Available at: https://youtu.be/Yw1cFk8vSs8

Chapter 2
Curran, T (2018) 'Our dangerous obsession with perfectionism is getting worse.'
Available at: https://youtu.be/lFG1b1-EsW8

Chapter 4
Holford, P. (2007) *Optimum Nutrition For The Mind.* Piatkus. Great Britain.

Mental Health Foundation UK (2021) 'Stress: statistics.
Available at:
https://www.mentalhealth.org.uk/explore-mental-health/statistics/stress-statistics

Chapter 5
National Center For Health Research (2018) 'Social Media and Adolescents' and Young Adults Mental Health.
Available at:
https://www.center4research.org/social-media-affects-mental-health/

Chapter 9

Daisley, B (2018) 'How laughter makes you a better worker'.
Available at:
https://www.bbc.com/worklife/article/20180404-how-laughter-makes-you-a-better-worker

Ghosh, P (2011) 'Study reveals laughter really is the best medicine'
Available at:
https://www.bbc.co.uk/news/science-environment-14889165

Chapter 11
The Therapeutic power of writing (2019) Available at:
https://www.bbc.co.uk/bitesize/articles/zbty6v4

Mental Health Foundation UK (2021) 'Nature: How connecting with nature helps our mental health.
Available at:
https://www.mentalhealth.org.uk/our-work/research/nature-how-connecting-nature-benefits-our-mental-health

Printed in Great Britain
by Amazon